LAST BEST YEAR

A SHORT GUIDE TO A GRATEFUL LIFE

ENDORSEMENTS

This gift book is truly a treasure. Wyland's clever snippets capture our thoughts and emotions, putting on the page what we all want and need. This book left me with a hope and lightheartedness.

—**Rachel Hauck**, *New York Times* bestselling author

In this beautiful book filled with faith and truth, Donna Wyland inspires us to live life to the fullest as we embrace the richness and beauty of the world around us. Readers will be encouraged to live each day with a mindset of gratitude, contentment, and joy, to follow their dreams, and invest in relationships that matter. Her words will motivate readers to love deeper, hug tighter, laugh harder, and give more generously. Those who follow her advice to rest, relax, and breathe will experience indescribable peace. I might be reading this book multiple times!

—**Crystal Bowman**, bestselling, award-winning author of more than 100 books including *I Love You to the Stars—When Grandma Forgets, Love Remembers*

It's often the little things in life that are the big things. In this delightful and heartwarming

"little" book, award-winning author Donna Wyland offers big truths that, if applied, will literally transform your life. In her inimitable way of deeply touching hearts, Donna will touch yours in ways that will help you see yourself as God sees you, so you can love as God loves. I highly recommend this book to anyone searching for true meaning in life.
—**MaryAnn Diorio**, PhD, MFA, novelist and life coach.

What would you do if you had only one year to live? Donna Wyland explores this profound question with depth and grace, offering readers a soulful journey of self-reflection. Her book inspires us to imagine and prioritize what truly matters in life. It's a powerful call to action, challenging us to reevaluate how we live each day with purpose and clarity. This book left me deeply moved, inspired to cherish every moment and align my actions with what I value most.
—**Dawn Damon**, award-winning author, international speaker

Too often it's the little things in life we take for granted. But as award-winning author Donna Wyland shows us through her beautiful words and photographs, it's those small moments we live for in the end.

Her new book, *Last Best Year*, takes us on a journey, inspiring us to reflect and use the strengths God has blessed us with to brighten the lives of others. Because we all know sharing with and encouraging others to be happy truly makes us happy.

—Ginny Simone, Award-winning journalist, former news anchor

Even though we are not always conscious of time fleeting by, the Bible says our days were numbered before one of them came to be. The stark truth is every one of our lifespans are finite. But imagine being given a sudden diagnosis of one year to live. After the initial shock, how would your life change? Donna Wyland has thought about that. In her sweet book, *Last Best Year*, she imagines how her priorities would change when knowing the end is in sight. She asks her readers: what would you do with one remaining year? It is a lovely read, thoughtful and warm. Peace and joy shine on every page. This one is a keeper!

—Julie Zine Coleman, Managing editor of the Arise Daily devotional website, author of *Unexpected Love: God's Heart Revealed Through Jesus's Conversations with Women* and *On Purpose: Discover God's Freedom for Women Through Scripture*

LAST BEST YEAR

A SHORT GUIDE TO A GRATEFUL LIFE

DONNA WYLAND

COPYRIGHT NOTICE

Cover and Interior Design: Kelly Artieri, Deb Haggerty
Editor(s): Peggy Ellis, Judy Hagey, Deb Haggerty
Photo Credits: See Appendix 1

PUBLISHED BY: Elk Lake Publishing, Inc., 35 Dogwood Drive, Plymouth, MA 02360, 2025

Library Cataloging Data
Names: Wyland, Donna (Donna Wyland)
Last Best Year: A Short Guide to a Grateful Life / Donna Wyland
84 p. 23cm × 15cm (9in × 6 in.)
ISBN-13: 9798891343641 (paperback) | 9798891343658 (trade paperback) | 9798891343665 (ebook)
Key Words: Women Christian living gift book photos faith; Christian self-help book testimony pictures prayer; Self-reflection grief recovery inspiration Jesus; Women empowerment relationship with God healing; Spirituality self-help Christian women's issues; Personal growth Biblical wisdom faith overcoming; Identity forgiveness redemption Christian living
Library of Congress Control Number: 2025937672 Nonfiction

For Papa

And to my parents who modeled for me the art of gratitude for little things. The joy they exuded while swinging on their 40th anniversary still brings a smile to my face. Their love lives on.

FOREWORD

Last Best Year—A Short Guide to a Grateful Life is an inspirational book inviting the reader to pause and ponder the question, "What would I do if I knew I had only one year to live?"

This book is deeply personal to me because there was a time in my life when I was diagnosed with a brain tumor doctors believed, at first, was inoperable. At that time, I faced the very same question.

Throughout this meaningful book, Donna captured so many of my own thoughts and emotions, which, years ago, I could not find the words to express fully. I laughed and cried as I read each page and appreciated so much the way she wrote this message with grace and eloquence about gratitude for everything, from the simplest blessing to the miraculous.

As Donna's words of encouragement flowed from the pages of this book into my heart, I relived those moments with heightened emotions of inexpressible joy and gratitude for the gift of another day, for tender moments when I could look into my son's blue eyes "one more time," for the gift of hearing my loved ones' voices, seeing another sunset, and eating a slice (or several slices) of my mom's German chocolate cake.

What I appreciated most about reading this book is how Donna's words consistently honor God, the Creator, Jesus, the Savior, and the Holy Spirit, our great Comforter. During the time after my diagnosis, I lived out many of the beautiful moments described vividly in this book.

I am deeply grateful to Donna for giving me the opportunity to be reminded of God's kindness and the peace and joy that come from living a daily life filled with gratitude. My cup runs over. May you find peace, encouragement, and inspiration as you read this book and are gently reminded of the many blessings that flow to and through a heart filled with gratitude.

—Janice LaVore-Fletcher, PCC, CMC, founder and president, The Christian Coach Institute, author, *Called to Coach—50 Inspirational Stories of Christian Coaches Who Answered God's Call*

PREFACE

What would you do if you were told you had one year to live? Pray for a miracle would be at the top of my list. I would want to be healed.

But what if God's desire was to take you home? What if the "days ordained for you," as written in Psalm 139, were about to end? Would you act differently? Think different thoughts? Would you feel like you lived a life of purpose *on* purpose or like you just lived?

The truth is, we don't know if we have one year, one month, or one day left on earth. In a *perfect* scenario, that uncertainty would compel us to live deeper, richer, more meaningful lives. But we all know there is just one place where perfection reigns.

This short essay is an inspiring message describing how a life might be lived with gratitude as its central theme. I pray this simple message will lead you to ponder the way you look at yourself and the world around you and to encourage you to consider what is possible for you today.

ACKNOWLEDGMENTS

Despite its brevity, this book has been several years in the making. When I first wrote the draft, I had just come out of a long period of emotional pain, and the primary thoughts of my mind and heart were centered on gratitude, and how thankful I was to finally be free. As life resumed with a new routine, I moved several times, leaving unopened boxes stacked in the garage or basement of whatever house I was renting at the time.

Fortunately, God healed my heart and led me to revisit this book with a renewed sense of gratitude. Having recently lost both of my parents and my husband's mother in the span of ten and a half months, I realize more fully how blessed we are to awaken each day, and how vital it is to appreciate the smallest gifts. I am humbled to see this book in print and pray, as you read it, you will be inspired to find your own personal joy each day.

I must begin by thanking my husband for his unwavering support of my writing, though it sometimes takes time from him and leaves him alone to watch football or golf or anything else he might be inclined to tune into. Gary, I am grateful for you. You are always on my side, even if it means sitting for hours at a book table helping me sell the books God has put on my heart to write. Thank you for everything. I will love you for all eternity.

To my four gorgeous daughters, Jennifer, Jessica, Lauren, and Nicole: you have taught me much about the art of gratitude as we've blended our families the past eight years. It hasn't been easy, but with a heart full of love and determination to bring us together as often as possible, we have begun to form something that is beautiful, unbreakable, and filled with hope. I love watching each of you grow into the graceful, intelligent women you were created to be.

To my husband's fun-loving family: you have embraced me in ways I never thought possible. Your Italian heritage and openly extroverted personalities have pulled me time and again out of my introverted writer's shell and shown me that love can be shared in unique and wonderful ways. I love all of you so much and pray we have many more years together (though you may need to visit me in the mountains during the hot, humid Florida summers).

Thank you, Deb Haggerty, Publisher & Editor in Chief of Elk Lake Publishing, Inc., for taking a chance on this unknown author so many years ago, and for giving me a voice in the busy world of publishing. You have blessed me more than you know by valuing the stories God has given me to write and encouraging me to continue this path of putting words on the page. I am forever grateful to you.

Peggy Ellis, you are an artful editor with a keen eye. You have kept me on track while other responsibilities clamored for my attention, and you have made this book stronger because of your efforts. Thank you for your patience and grace throughout this process. I think we created a beautiful book with a powerful, meaningful message.

Janice LaVore-Fletcher, you are my Crazy Christian Sister Chick, and I love you more than words can say. You have been the wind beneath my wings and my constant encouragement and guide. Thank you for sharing your heart in this book's Foreword and for loving me through the many ups and downs of my life. Your heart for Christ and desire to bless others will forever remind me of what is truly worth living for. You inspire me to reach higher and go deeper, and for that, I will always be grateful.

Ginny Simone, dear friend of mine, you are accomplished in your own right as a former news anchor for several large markets across the United States, yet you took time to read this manuscript and encourage me to submit it for publication. Your constant positivity is infectious, and your friendship is much appreciated. Thank you for sharing your heart and life with me.

Lynne Marie Davis, Erin MacLellan, Claudia Newton, Debbie Rasa, Rebecca Kendrick, Kerri Goodman, Marty Palmer, Connie Corrova, Cindy Johnson, Hollie D'Agata, Laura Hoogerhyde, Dawn Scott Damon, Julie Coleman, MaryAnn Diorio, Crystal Bowman, Rachel Hauck, the Ladies of AWSA Mastermind, Jeanne Rock, Beth Capozzelli, and Joan Templer: Each of you has encouraged me in many different ways and helped me during the difficult times to stay strong and trust that all will be well. Without you, my life would not know true friendship and grace. Thank you all for being the kind of friends I can be authentic and honest with. Our connection runs deep. I am grateful for your constant love and support.

To fellow authors who wrote endorsements for *Last Best Year*—Rachel Hauck, Dawn Damon, Julie Coleman, Crystal Bowman, MaryAnn Diorio, and Ginny Simone—I am grateful for your time and words of affirmation. With each book I write, I wonder, "Will others be blessed and drawn closer to God through it?" Your endorsements affirm that God is, indeed, in my heart and in my work. There is no greater goal in life than to bring others closer to the One who lives in us. Thank you for confirming I am doing just that.

To my parents who passed within seven months of one another, one through tragedy, the other because of dementia and heart issues, I am grateful for your gift of wisdom. You were always thankful for the little things. That was a powerful lesson for me to learn. I pray you are looking down from heaven, delighting as I play with words, enjoy life, and remember you with great love and tenderness. Mom, you were, and your memory will always be, my true north.

Last, I thank Gerald Joseph Grillo, Sr. (Jerry to friends and "Papa" to the Grillo family) for showing me how to find joy in simple things. At ninety-six years old, you continue to share your unique blend of intelligence, humor, and musical talent with those of us who are blessed to know you. I love you more each day and cherish every moment we are together. Despite the aches, pains, and challenges of macular degeneration, you are gratitude in motion—the reason I believe in the possibility of living a joy-filled life after ninety—or even one hundred! Everyone has bad days, but you know how to rise above. Thank you for showing me what "aging gracefully" really means.

LAST BEST YEAR

If I Had One Year to Live

If I had one year to live, I would slide the bedroom curtains off their rods and awaken with the sun each day. If the sky was filled with clouds, I would close my eyes and envision the light above the gray. I would brew a cup of coffee or tea and race to the porch to shout *Good Morning!* to the God who created all things and blessed me with another day.

Rain or shine, I would declare each day a most wonderful gift. And I would learn to be content with moments, events, and people who are less than perfect, because aren't we all imperfect? We are spiritual souls in human bodies learning how to bring love and joy to the world while we are here. I would want people to feel greater joy and more deeply loved after spending time with me.

I would learn to forgive and move on. Forgive the girl in high school who stole not one, but two of my boyfriends. Forgive my parents for not letting me go to certain parties, and thank them for protecting me from trouble. Forgive my husband for disappointing me so often, and forgive myself for carrying such high expectations into our marriage that he was doomed to fail before we said I Do. Forgive. Let go. Be free.

FOLLOW YOUR
DREAMS

I would embrace a new hobby I have been too afraid to try, fearing I might fail. I would accept the fact I will never pitch a perfect game of horseshoe or ace a top-ranked tennis star. I will never bowl a 300 or quilt a king-sized comforter by hand. I will never be a royal queen or accomplish many other dreams my young mind imagined. I would free myself of competitive thoughts and worry and envy, and oh, those unrealistic expectations, so I could authentically experience all the world has to offer. I would dare to follow my dreams—allowing them to lead me down an unknown path—and I would vow to love each moment and every fearful step.

I would cherish moments with my mom and dad, and spend more time with friends whose unconditional love for me has filled my heart and led me to feel like they are family too. I would forget any attempts at being the favorite daughter or cousin or coworker because, in the end, all that matters is we love well and try to be the best human being that we can be. Give and receive. Open our heart wider and repeat.

I would pray for everyone to come to know the Creator of life and the world we inhabit. I would stop searching for comfort and happiness by living small, because life would be colorless and boring without victories *and* defeats, elation *and* despair. I would thank God for creating a multidimensional world where struggles and failures can lead to unparalleled adventure, growth, success, and enough positivity to influence multitudes of people to take a risk and step out of their comfort zones too.

I would give more than I take and volunteer for the smallest tasks—like listening to a child read and folding brochures at a nonprofit. I would realize I have always had more than I need, and I could give so much more than I have given, because giving is about more than money. I have talents to share and time to spare and treasure that includes giving my heart.

If I had one year to live, I would love deeper, listen closer, and give friends and loved ones my full attention. I would live in the moment and learn to appreciate the sound of children playing in the yard, no matter how loud they got, because children represent life and energy, and purity of heart. How could I despise that? I was once one of the loudest voices in the crowd.

I would only watch movies that make me laugh because laughter—the deep belly kind—is believed to prolong a person's life, and in some instances, unequivocally save it. I would want to give myself every chance to live. Besides, if I died during a scary movie, my face would be covered in shock, and that's not my best look. I would rather die with a smile on my face and wrinkles beside each of my eyes, a testimony to a heart filled with joy.

I would believe in the power of God and the hope of heaven. I would pore over books that lift my spirit in positive ways and fill me with inspiration, encouragement, and hope. I would soak up every word that has been written to describe eternity's wonder and beauty, and I would close my eyes and try with all my might to envision how truly breathtaking heaven will be.

If I had one year to live, I would surround myself with colors, shapes, sounds, and tastes that whisper sweetness to my soul. I would sleep in the softest sheets and wear the softest silk pajamas, pretending to be privileged and proper. If I have a roof over my head, clothes to wear, and food to eat, I *am* privileged, compared to much of the world's population.

I would encourage others more and attempt to help them discover their own unique gifts and talents. I would prove they have no reason to be afraid of being outrun by someone better, stronger, or faster, because the world is big enough for everyone to perform at their highest level without pushing others down.

I would swing at a school and skip through the park, maybe even take up birding or participate in a nature hike or wildflower walk. I have never been much into those types of activities, but if I had one year to live, I would want to do it all, discover everything I could, probe the minds of intelligent people, seeking answers to the questions I've long pondered in my mind. Sometimes I would just want to *be*. Rest. Relax. Breathe.

If I had one year to live, I would devour ice cream with chocolate sauce and sliced bananas for breakfast, and enjoy pizza with extra cheese whenever I craved it—which is most days. I love cheese! After all those nature hikes and wildflower walks, I could afford the extra calories. Who would be counting?

I would laugh more at myself and at everything that tickles my funny bone. I would teach people the only joke I know how to tell, so they could make others laugh too. Having the humility to look at ourselves and recognize the humor when we mess up, or even act silly on purpose, is one of the most desirable traits we can possess. Laughter lowers our defenses and connects us to one another in a significant way.

I would stop blaming my husband, parents, boss, kids, and others for the circumstances of my life and accept the path I lived was the path I chose to take. Every thought, word, and choice led me to where I am today. The buck truly does stop with me, but I retain the right to create a new life by thinking positive thoughts, speaking encouraging words, and making choices based on advice, wisdom, and prayer. I would feel proud of my accomplishments, grateful God's definition of success is the opposite of the world's.

I would hug children and pet animals (except big dogs—I'm afraid of them but am willing to learn to try to love them too) and absorb every scent and sight around me. I would not live with abandon, but with the purpose of desiring to leave this world having resolved past issues, healed wounds and traumas, and opened new vistas for myself and others. Every day would be devoted to loving better and embracing others' differences with curiosity, kindness, and hope.

If I had one year to live, I would bequeath as much as I could to charity, specifically those whose work I am most familiar with, and who make the greatest impact on the lives of those in need. I would inform my family and friends of my decision and challenge them to do the same.

I would not weigh myself or stand in front of the mirror looking for wrinkles, rolls, and bulges. I would be grateful to have breathed—to have lived at all—and I would proclaim myself to be at peace with who I am. I would decide to be happy growing old with grace—not a surgically taut face.

I would write a letter to my family to apologize for my wrongs and shower them with praise for what they did right. I would pour out my heart and list the many reasons I love them. I would share warm salty fries and thick creamy shakes without worrying about getting my fair share. And I would lend my clothes to any friend in need without expecting them to be returned.

If I had one year to live, I would lounge by a fire in the middle of June or shimmy into a swimsuit in January to sit in a hot tub while snowflakes floated from the sky. Whatever my mood, I would find a way to fulfill my desires as best I could, knowing it would make me happy, and a happy person is more likely to make *others* happy. Who doesn't want to be remembered as someone who did that?

I would learn to paint the simplest things, and I would hang them where everyone could see, not to be complimented or commented on, but to bless myself and the world around me by sharing my gratitude and creativity through my humble works of art.

I would think before I speak and return emails and letters in a timely manner. I might even commit to snail mail, sending cards and hand-written letters. They become treasures to the ones we leave behind—the items gently bundled and wrapped in thin satin ribbon to be fondled, reread, and shared with distant relatives for generations to come.

If I had one year to live, I would ponder the mountaintops and valleys, simple pleasures and amazing adventures. I would try to sum them up in one short sentence to describe what my life meant to me—a phrase for my tombstone—something like, *She was lost, and then found not only herself, but the secret to living well.*

I would let everyone who read my epitaph wonder what that secret was, which truly is not a secret at all.

Living well is a gift, a glimpse of heaven to come. We don't find peace and happiness within ourselves. Ultimate joy is found in relationship with God, the source of all life. Loving and serving others is a close second, helping humanity by sharing our talents and gifts.

What we reap, we truly do sow. This is not just a paraphrase of a famous quote, but a profound soul truth personified in agricultural terminology.

There are so many things I would do if I had one year to live, but above all, I would want to love others to the best of my ability. And I would allow them to love me in return, because I want to die with a full heart and leave a legacy of love behind me.

ABOUT THE AUTHOR

Donna Wyland is an award-winning author, editor, and ICF-certified coach. Two of her picture books, *Psalms in Rhyme for Little Hearts* and *'Twas the Night Before Jesus* were Readers' Choice Award Finalists. In addition, *'Twas the Night Before Jesus* won the 2025 Illumination Award Silver Medal, and *Psalms in Rhyme for Little Hearts* won the 2024 Christian Indie Award.

She was recognized by *Writer's Digest* for her poetry, and she won Writer of the Year at the Florida Christian Writer's Conference in 2018 where she was awarded top honors for her devotionals, humor, poetry, and flash fiction. She has written for *Clubhouse, Jr.*, *Focus on the Family*, and *Story Friends* magazines, and she has contributed personal essays and poems to numerous publications.

Donna's books have been gifted to thousands of children around the world through Military Ministry of Campus Crusade for Christ, All God's Children International, The Library of Hope, Manners of the Heart Community Fund, and many other individuals and organizations. Her picture books were also featured at a book signing at the Pentagon in Arlington, Virginia.

Donna has traveled extensively to international destinations and loves meeting people from all cultures. She is a former lay counselor and worship singer, and she has shared her testimony with women's groups in various churches across the United States.

She writes in her home office in Southwest Florida and dreams of learning Italian and French to prepare her for more trips to faraway places around the world.

LIST OF PHOTOS

- Cover Photo #1, Author Photo of parents on their 40th wedding anniversary
- Photo #2, Photo of myself with my father-in-law for Dedication Page.
- Photo #3, Woman with coffee mug in gray sweater in morning sunlight. #391429462
- Photo #4, Girls at sunset with "heart hands" #262835786
- Photo #5, Woman with outstretched arms (release, freedom) #789907663
- Photo #6, Path with "Follow Your Dreams" #171818625
- Photo #7, Heart in hands in sand. #797559169
- Photo #8, Stairs toward heavenly light #829759619
- Photo #9, Older woman reading to child # 492105981
- Photo #10, Children having fun on rope swing #244216786
- Photo #11, People laughing. #790339978
- Photo #12, Hands praying with Bible #360077416

- Photo #13, Woman asleep in bed #603057235
- Photo #14, Person standing on mountain top #767557954
- Photo #15, Woman with eyes closed lying on grass #485571190
- Photo #16, Milkshake on diner countertop #805159310
- Photo #17, Elderly couple laughing on bench #599256231
- Photo #18, Sun shining through trees #925477974
- Photo #19, Young girl holding dog #681693125
- Photo #20, Woman with "Volunteer" on T-shirt #493187376
- Photo #21, Headshot of woman with gray hair in rain jacket #667266509
- Photo #22, Handwriting a letter #199554465
- Photo #23, Young couple in hot tub in winter #986689542
- Photo #24, Author Photo of family's artwork hanging in my office
- Photo #25, Stack of letters and old photographs #943012476
- Photo #26, Winding mountain road through lush valley #797972093

- Photo #27, Keyhole-shaped doorway with light shining through #329760982

- Photo #28, Sunlight shining through clouds #844034040

- Photo #29, Author Photo—Grillo (Wyland) family at daughter's wedding

Pictures with nine-digit numbers secured from Adobe Stock Photos (stock.adobe.com).

OTHER BOOKS BY DONNA WYLAND

- *Autumn's Harmony*
- *Surrender*
- *A Guided Gratitude Journal*

Books for Children

- *'Twas the Night Before Jesus*
- *Psalms in Rhyme for Little Hearts*
- *If I Could Ask Jesus*
- *Your Home in Heaven*